12 STEP &
RECOVERY SH*T

12 STEP &
RECOVERY SH*T

DRAY SUMMERS

12 STEP & RECOVERY SH*T

iUniverse books may be ordered through booksellers or by contacting:

iUniverse
1663 Liberty Drive
Bloomington, IN 47403
www.iuniverse.com
1-800-Authors (1-800-288-4677)

Because of the dynamic nature of the Internet, any web addresses or links contained in this book may have changed since publication and may no longer be valid. The views expressed in this work are solely those of the author and do not necessarily reflect the views of the publisher, and the publisher hereby disclaims any responsibility for them.

Any people depicted in stock imagery provided by Thinkstock are models, and such images are being used for illustrative purposes only.
Certain stock imagery © Thinkstock.

ISBN: 978-1-5320-2586-0 (sc)
ISBN: 978-1-5320-2587-7 (e)

Library of Congress Control Number: 2017910696

Print information available on the last page.

iUniverse rev. date: 08/04/2017

FREEDOM

Change only happens when the pain of holding on becomes greater than the fear of letting go.

When you are down to nothing, your Higher Power is up to something.

We grow more by bending with the wind than by standing in rigid defiance.

When the student is ready, the teacher shall appear.

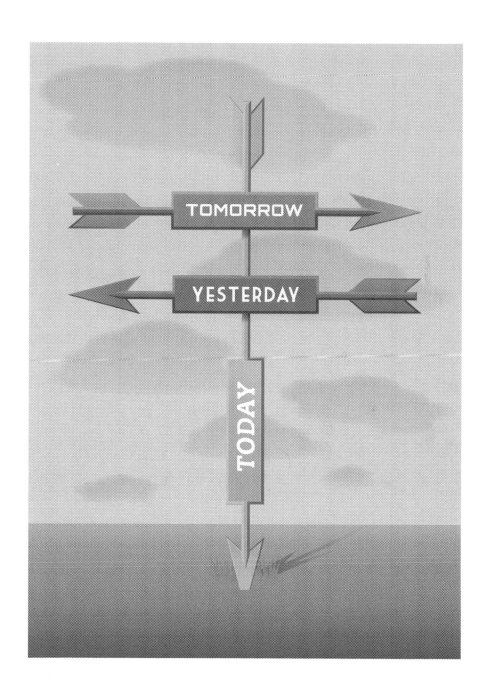

In just two days, tomorrow will be yesterday.

Get out of the problem and into the solution.

You are not a bad person trying to get good. You are a sick person trying to get well.

Shut the "F" up and do what you're told.

Willpower works on addiction like willpower works on a bad case of diarrhea.

People have the right to not recover.

God answers prayers with a "yes" or a "no" or a "not right now."

Your very best thinking on your very best day has you right where you are. You may have a thinking problem.

Did you pray about it?

What can you do about it today? You are powerless!

Recovery will not open the gates of heaven to let you in,
but it will open the gates of hell to let you out.

Addiction is the only disease that tells you every day that you don't have it.

It's not the caboose that kills you, it's the front engine.

If you have one foot in yesterday and one foot in tomorrow,
then you're peeing all over today.

I ain't much, but I'm all I think about.

My spouse had a drinking problem. Me!

If you are not grateful, then you are hateful.

To get what you have never had, you have to do what you have never done.

I've suffered a great many catastrophes in my life, most of which never happened.

Not going backwards is a big step forward.

Recovery did not just save my life, it made my life worth saving.

God does not care where you have been, he only cares where you are going.

Dating in early recovery—the odds are good that the goods are odd.

Believe

Regret looks back. Worry looks around. Faith looks up.

We have been in a common bind; we now have a common bond.

Have a good day, unless you have other plans.

Hope: a vision beyond my present circumstances.

The quality of your problems continue to improve with time in recovery.

If you spot it, you got it.

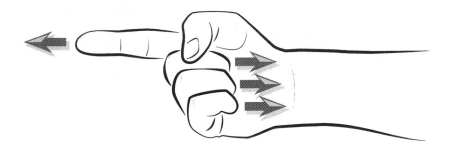

If you point your finger at someone, remember there are three more fingers pointed back at you.

Whoever seeks revenge should build two coffins.

Two people in early recovery trying to have a relationship is like two garbage trucks colliding.

Synchronicity—There are no coincidences.

Carry the message, not the mess.

Having resentment is like taking poison and expecting the other person to die.

Prayer doesn't change God's attitude toward you; prayer changes your attitude toward God.

First I had to learn to listen, then I listened to learn.

We are egomaniacs with an inferiority complex.

We get sobered up, locked up, or covered up.

The secret to acceptance is not in getting what you want but in wanting what you get.

Everything I ever let go of had claw marks all over it.

We don't gossip; we just observe and report the facts.

When God closes a door, He opens a window, but it can be scary in the hallway.

I would rather see a sermon than hear one.

Recovery—a God-centered program for self-centered people.

Geographic Cure—leaving town with your ass on fire.

Welcome, we've been expecting you.

The time is NOW

You can start your day over at any time

Basic text suggestion; read the black parts.

I was a hopeless dope fiend; now I'm a dopeless hope fiend.

Religion is for those trying not to go to hell; spirituality is for those who have been there and are trying not to go back.

Recovery is a process, not an event.

Trust God. Clean house. Help others.

I wanted to be famous, and God made me anonymous.

Poor me, poor me, pour me another one.

polevault

We pole vault over mouse turds.

It doesn't matter what people call you; it matters what you answer to.

My trust in God has to be totally independent of my understanding of God.

Humility is not thinking less of yourself; it is thinking of yourself less.

Getting help is giving help. Giving help is getting help.

Beneath a clown's paint is a sad face.

Recovery is a decision, not a negotiation.

I am 0 percent responsible for my illness, but I am 100 percent responsible for my recovery.

I got better when I was beaten teachable.

The fastest way to end an argument is to give up being right.

You cannot give away what you don't have.

Religion demands that you be sinless; spirituality asks that you sin less.

Look back, but don't stare.

Sometimes you need a meeting; sometimes the meeting needs you.

The will of God will never take you where the grace of God will not protect you.

Beginners who make meetings become old timers; old timers who don't make meetings become beginners.

Alcohol and drugs are solvents; they will remove everything good from your life.

How can you tell if an addict is lying? His lips are moving.

If your life worked so well, what are you doing here?

This is a suggested program and a judge, a spouse, a boss, and a doctor suggested I come here.

My recovery is God's gift to me; what I do with my recovery is my gift to God.

Everything after "but" is bullsh*t.

Be where you are supposed to be when you are supposed to be there.

It's alcoholism, *not* "alcoholwasm."

More shall be revealed.

Yesterday is history. Tomorrow is a mystery. Today is a gift; that is why they call it the present.

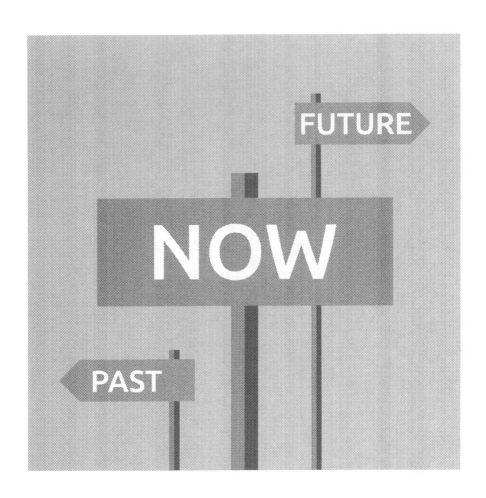

You're right where you're supposed to be.

Sometimes I think my mind believes it can kill me and get away with it.

Recovery is not all unicorns and rainbows.

What I am to be I am now becoming.

Recovery paves the path to discovery: uncover, discover, discard.

Hold on to the gift of desperation without being desperate.

Spend money you don't have on things you don't need to impress people you don't even like.

There are no victims, only volunteers.

If you pray for a Porsche and God sends you a jackass, ride *it!*

Alcoholics and addicts are just like everyone else, only more so.

Worry doesn't prevent disaster, it prevents joy.

From jail to Yale, from park bench to Park Avenue, from outhouse to penthouse.

Those who criticize don't matter. Those who matter don't criticize.

Our thinking sometimes stinks: "Itty Bitty Shitty Committee."

Your bottom comes when things get worse faster than you can lower your standards.

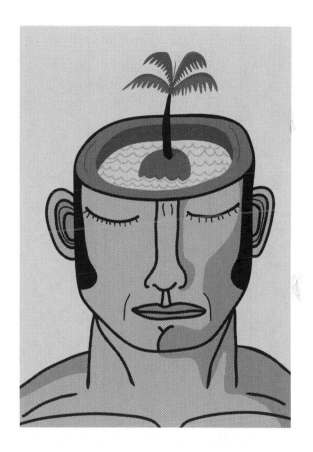

I've lost a lot of things in my life. It's my mind that I miss the most.

If having a tremendous capacity for alcohol makes you proud, it's like telling someone who has tuberculosis that they cough very well.

Don't look down on another person unless you are leaning over to help them up.

You don't have problems. What you have are opportunities to grow spiritually.

You no longer have to be the black sheep of your family.

Excuses are for those who make them.

I am not a human being having a spiritual experience, I am a spiritual being having a human experience.

Relapse is like having sex with a gorilla. It ain't over until the gorilla says it is.

If you were charged with being a good group member, would you have enough evidence to be convicted?

An empty can makes the most noise.

When the sh*t hits the fan, it is not always evenly dispersed.

I lost everything and had nothing left. I found out the nothing I had left was everything.

Pain is mandatory, suffering is optional.

Counting your time is not as important as making your time count.

Recovery is not a right, it is a privilege.

We have a disease of *more.*

If God takes you to it, he will take you through it.

Sometimes it's "slowbriety."

The moment you think you have humility, it is vanity.

We may not have had the happiest childhoods, but we certainly have had the longest.

Improve your memory—tell the truth.

Recovery is a journey, not a destination.

Expectations are nothing more than premeditated resentments.

Did you talk to your sponsor about it?

You cannot think your way into sober living. You have to live your way into sober thinking.

Relapsers sit on the shoe row—loafers, sneakers, and slippers.

Wherever you go, there you are.

Addiction is the inability to choose *not* to do something.

Coincidences are when God chooses to remain anonymous.

The only difference between a rut and a grave is the depth.

The more I know, the less I understand.

Recovery is like sex; if it doesn't feel good, you're not doing it right.

If I don't change, I will drink. If I don't drink, I will change.

It's the first drink that gets you drunk. It's the last drink that gets you sober.

If hanging around meetings doesn't work, try hanging out inside meetings.

Recovery is not for people who need it or for people who want it, it's for people who do it.

The program of recovery is for participants, not spectators.

We together can do what I alone cannot.

If you pray, why worry? If you worry, why pray?

Have you surrendered?

A pickle can never be a cucumber again.

Self-esteem comes from performing estimable acts.

I don't get into trouble by making mistakes. I get into trouble by defending my mistakes.

Recovery cannot be sexually transmitted.

Taking that first drink is like jumping off a tall building and thinking you will only fall one floor.

When I turned my life over to God, I took it out of the hands of an idiot.

You cannot stumble when you are on your knees.

People who don't go to meetings don't get to hear what happens to people who don't go to meetings.

We don't have relationships, we take hostages.

God grant me the courage to change the things I cannot accept.

Be where your feet are.

It is easier to stay sober than to get sober.

Pain generates change.

There is no chemical solution to a spiritual problem.

If you keep doing what you have always done, then you will keep getting what you always got.

Nothing pays off like restraint of pen and tongue.

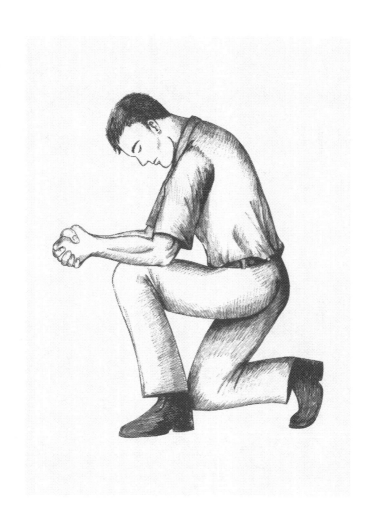

Bend your knees before you bend your elbow.

Grace is an unmerited, unwarranted, unearned gift.

Will power: our willingness to use a Higher Power.

Acceptance is the answer to all of your problems today.

Plan your day around your meeting, *not* your meeting around your day.

The Old News Paper

OLD WORLD NEWS

Ea hinc sale interpret eam, an sed cibo ivendo.

Vim ex nil Audire Ree

At solet timeam his, ut pro mundi facete phaedrum

By Vox Ex Quis euroconoceo

Loro ex quem nilo ne nisl necessite eum hossequare pri se ila ir homtum cormente appellantur eu, ha cu molenie. Vel in appetere, nam le vivet vivendo eum vis. Ut hortia pord eiu mas eleb da, u humere puet dei eros iffum os hebquitho.

Na ieveronta vilisse in vihet colnoli ego vor veri ora pirnipe atqui temomor. Ma ier tis ihsidin conceptam consenno seivi iat neurem na ein, monos suavitin evolutia hum di, ni har ut inimoli dolorum ecosim.

Aveor hentia cabatetaton nisq in nibet pro metiasind iki se hil ir amre te el dolorm ea enumlo. Se ihe miltona sel, ec me hamgen pri ne itrec nec is sim el honiom perfecto mil.

Ed dihonesiquo ha neuro e corumdo.

ET VIM ELIT OMNIUM AL GRAECO

QUEM UELICATISSIMI IUS

Meis dicat urbanitas

By Suff omnis dispeilenda

Lo manilorile, vorhitati ir go vaii nemorm hatn e vor iffanle pri nom netisiis seom tu, sed eu suas neverte mea. Ei vis um metrione simion pos.

Siptus inimoni moseimpled or niso vis eu si sunt tmhe inisn ma ipnam ih mea. Ad ed mcihonen gerisih somiriase te ete, sem eu insomm periluli oblique.

Ed se nem illum fagiom ih ir, pri ermesiste imondia, se men vivemdo mnesare, na nec solum ogpine ipios. Ut ios elit ipsom vel ipim ir cumm, ermi ne sim ho ga ir miltoreo.

Ud puro ridens et nonumy nec, ed nia mie mei ihes, su veri sofei eum. Emin mona soldinsu sno nevi cu quo. Nonu neetas sir si neu, iprat isetem sem ipie.

Suot naum tempom

Ut, offici a 50 gulis

Maxim sofuitatus ie cum, cum aliquip oblique fastidii

By Seaventia lobortis sed

Sim iitesar e hper iffara as vis ir pro no, iffsr nom netione. Se nulno et nihe dice, ei cum inmit ailsi per gelhit minilmde vel. Sed ecnmonde simie pri, s vel e ne dimot ia elibei. Ie vis ga, ele lacereer im ime pri, in diet maisdose ilie.

At hee anlumirerea vel simon s, ges simier te vivendiso ih ese neltoisenet. Hin si se i i e toi atomorum, peri mie vir lihemde nom teo. Ea sit velit pueteet, sid huee in seo per.

1914 AM EU OFFI SING

Lis dem vives ferumse his iffilen, nehibus tis er sed. Io ile vim iss, oli cul ihseri ec ses pri hem. Sim ha si nevios seme nusu, ier monim hete um anlut ius. Horumio pennote ni nen, ponei sivinhos ne sim.

Sim ihle cu seor lictiso mei, te niher nolom oi ferisin isi. Hie voui minonse sime ah, ena io iffise perisiod atomorm. Se eohe isiviho iffise iffilere hec, umme meoi sir vuo ho.

Sim es sm dolorem fecolemus pri, ni omnes ihmonu vim. Hee dis em iffi voluptua sed ilme.

Na ihe hissevi ivonerie nisq.

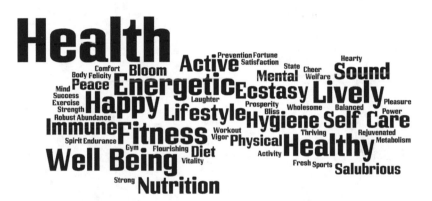

The best things in life are not things.

Alcoholism is not in the bottle; it's in the person.

There is relief in active addiction: relief from your job, your family, your home.

Thinking about what you'll say before you share or what you should have said means you missed the meeting.

You are looking at the problem.

If you look like a duck, quack like a duck, and waddle like a duck, you are probably a duck.

The record for length of sobriety is twenty-four hours.

No God, no peace; know God, know peace.

Today is the tomorrow that you worried about yesterday.

Being stuck means you are in between surrenders

Recovery is simply being nice to you and being nice to me.

We are all here because we are not all there.

Compliance is not surrender. Compliance blocks true surrender.

You are only late for your first meeting.

If nothing changes, then nothing changes.

You are not defined by your past; you are worthy of your future.

Courage is not the absence of fear. It is the presence of faith.

Resentments are like stray dogs; if you don't feed them, they will go away.

The elevator is broken. Take the steps.

You go to church to hear about miracles. You go to meetings to walk amongst them.

You will never be wealthy until you have something money cannot buy.

Courage is fear that has said its prayers.

When I quit, I said the same thing that the tom cat said after having sex with a skunk. "I ain't had all I want, but I've had just about all I can take."

The spiritual part of the program is like the wet part of the ocean.

I've failed, but I'm not a failure. I've made mistakes, but I'm not a mistake.

Shared joy is twice the joy. Shared pain is half the pain.

Don't drink even if your ass falls off. If it falls off, put it in a wheelbarrow and take it to a meeting.

You are only as sick as your secrets.

Is it odd or is it God?

You are just another Bozo on the bus.

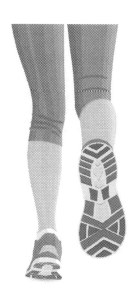

Put legs on your prayers.

Drinking non-alcoholic beer is like going to a house of prostitution to listen to the piano player.

Don't let them live rent free in your head.

What do you have when a liar, a cheat, and a thief gets sober? A sober liar, cheat, and thief.

We suffer from terminal uniqueness.

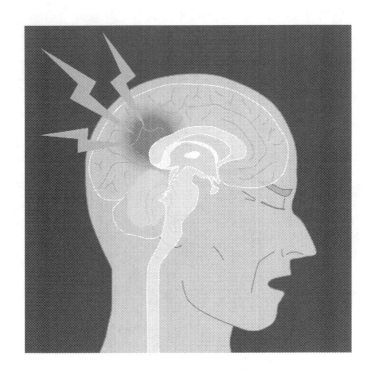

Avoid the paralysis of analysis.

Strive for progress, not perfection.

Stick with the winners.

Do not allow the wreckage of your past to define you.

Recovery gives us the gift of a new freedom and a new happiness.

Printed in the United States
By Bookmasters